S0-DYU-606

IS
THE
HOLY
SPIRIT
REAL?

IS THE HOLY SPIRIT REAL?

By

Dr. Paul E. Paino

Paul E. Paino Ministries, Inc.
P.O. Box 12205
Fort Wayne, Indiana USA 46863-2205

Unless otherwise indicated, all Scripture quotations are taken from the King James Version of the Bible.

IS THE HOLY SPIRIT REAL?

Copyright © 1992 Paul E. Paino Ministries, Inc.

ISBN 1-882357-01-9

Published by Paul E. Paino Ministries, Inc.
P.O. Box 12205, Fort Wayne, IN 46863-2205

All rights reserved under International Copyright Law. This publication may not be reproduced, stored in a retrieval system, or transmitted in whole or in part, in any form or by any means, electronic, mechanical, photocopying, recording or otherwise, without the prior express written permission of the Publisher.

Printed in the United States of America.

DEDICATION

In Memory Of

I have written this booklet in memory of a precious man, my father, Rev. Thomas Paino, Sr.

He received the Baptism in the Holy Spirit in 1918 and preached the gospel in store fronts, gospel tents, brush arbors, and any other place that he could share the gospel. He built churches in city after city and built and pastored a great church in Indianapolis for over a half century.

He was a dedicated, loving and praying man who faithfully served the Lord. In his memory, I dedicate these pages.

INTRODUCTION

In 1923 I was born into a Pentecostal home. My father was mustered out of the Army after the armistice was signed in 1917. World War I had come to a close. Father was born in Italy and was nurtured and raised in the Roman Catholic Church. He served as an altar boy and was a member of the Knights of Columbus.

As a result of hearing a Methodist preacher preaching the gospel on the streets of a vacation town in the Adirondack Mountains, father received the Lord Jesus Christ as his personal Saviour. The Lord led him and his wife to Indianapolis where, for the first time, he witnessed people who had received the Baptism in the Holy Spirit. He saw their joy, and listened as they worshipped, praised, and prayed. He saw hundreds of people receive the Baptism in the Holy Spirit. The power of the Lord was demonstrated through many miraculous healings and deliverances.

Mrs. Mary Woodworth Etter was being mightily used of God in the ministry of divine healing. At the turn of the century, she wrote such books as *Questions* and *Answers on Divine Healing, Signs and Wonders,* and *Marvels and Miracles.* She was among the first to be so mightily used by the Holy Spirit in the outpouring that swept across the world in the early 1900's. Hundreds of people came to Indianapolis to attend the meetings. It was a time of refreshing from the Lord and a spirit of revival was sweeping across the land.

It was into this atmosphere that God directed my father. He received the Baptism in the Holy Spirit in 1920. I was born into the family three years later.

As men and women sought the Lord, they experienced a glorious "Baptism" into the Holy Spirit. It was always accompanied with the recipient **"speaking in other tongues."** People did not know, nor could they explain, what was happening; but, they knew that the Holy Spirit was doing a wonderful work in their hearts. Lives were changed. Miracles took place and the power of God was made known across the land. It was a sovereign move of God's Spirit. God poured His Spirit out at Azusa Street in California, in Topeka, Kansas, in upper New York State; and reports came from all around the world that this was "The Latter Rain." God had promised to pour out His Spirit upon all flesh in the "last days" and now it had started.

My father and mother were called into the ministry and began traveling with an old Model-T Ford, a trailer, and a gospel tent that would seat about one hundred and fifty people. They moved from community to community and built churches. They preached in Evansville, Indiana; Mount Carmel, Illinois; Danville, Illinois; Covington, Indiana; Linton, Indiana, etc. On and on they went carrying the glorious Pentecostal message.

It was a fourfold message. Jesus Christ was Saviour. Jesus Christ was Healer. Jesus Christ was Baptizer. Jesus Christ was a soon-coming King.

This was the message they preached in store fronts, in old gospel tents, under brush arbors, and in sawdust-floored tabernacles. The resistance was unbelievable. I can remember my father preaching when he would be pelted with tomatoes, cabbage, and anything else that could be thrown at him. His tent was cut down. The church he pastored was burned to the ground by vandals. People were called "holy rollers." The main-line denominations resisted the move of God's Spirit. Members who received the Baptism in the Holy Spirit were excommunicated and forced out of the fellowship. They were often rejected, ridiculed, and persecuted.

However, the work of God was real.

The fire was spreading. God was doing a new thing, and the Holy Spirit was preparing the church for its greatest outreach since the early outpouring at Pentecost. People were being "endued with power" to carry the gospel message to the four corners of the earth. It was a Pentecostal revival!! Wonderful things were happening. The power of God was manifested. Jesus Christ was glorified, and the gospel was preached to the four corners of the earth.

It was into this atmosphere that I was born and raised. These Spirit-filled believers did not own songbooks. There were few trained and educated preachers. They met wherever they could find a place to invite people and the work of the Spirit continued to spread from place to place.

There were excesses. Believers had come into a beautiful relationship with Jesus Christ by the power and ministry of the Holy Spirit. Many needed instruction and direction. Emotions were stirred and new-found joy and liberty flooded into the hearts of the people. There was great rejoicing. The power of God was present. A spirit of prayer fell upon hundreds of people and, as these believers sought the Lord, God continued to pour out His Spirit upon them.

As I grew older, I was always aware of the presence of the Holy Spirit. The Holy Spirit was honored in our home. My father preached on the subject "The Baptism in the Holy Spirit"; and he led hundreds and hundreds of people into the experience. God had blessed him with a special anointing to pray over believers and rejoice when they would break forth glorifying the Lord in their "spirit language."

Mother had the heart and spirit of an evangelist. When she preached, people filled the altars seeking the Lord for salvation. It was a beautiful combination. Mother would preach people into the Kingdom, and Father would pray until they would receive the Baptism in the Holy Spirit.

While attending Bible school in the early 1940's, I began asking serious questions concerning the work, the ministry, and the personality of the Holy Spirit. Here are some questions with which I constantly wrestled:

(1) Do all believers in Jesus Christ receive the Holy Spirit?

(2) Does the Baptism in the Holy Spirit produce Christian character?

(3) Is the Baptism in the Holy Spirit primarily for the purpose of receiving power?

(4) Is there a difference between being baptized in the Spirit and being infilled with the Spirit??

(5) Does the experience of the Baptism give us power to witness or does receiving the Holy Spirit give us this power?

(6) What is the purpose of "tongues"?

(7) Can the "gifts of the Spirit" or "spirituals" operate in a person who has not received the Baptism in the Holy Spirit?

(8) Are all of the "spirituals" or "gifts of the Spirit" to operate in the local church today?

(9) Are these "spirituals" resident in the believer, and can these "gifts" function at the will or bidding of the believer?

These are a few of the questions that I want to address in the following pages. As a result of searching the Scriptures concerning these matters, the Lord gave me clear understanding concerning the work and ministry of the Holy Spirit.

Yes…the HOLY SPIRIT is **REAL!**

CONTENTS

Chapter One:
The Work of the Holy Spirit in Regeneration 1

Chapter Two:
The Work of the Holy Spirit in Infilling 17

Chapter Three:
The Work of the Holy Spirit in Anointing 25

Chapter Four:
The Work of the Holy Spirit in Baptism 35

CHAPTER ONE

THE WORK OF THE HOLY SPIRIT IN REGENERATION

No person can say that Jesus is Lord but by the Holy Spirit!

> *"...and that no man can say that Jesus is the Lord but by the Holy Ghost."*
> *I Corinthians 12:3b*

It is the Holy Spirit that convicts and convinces of sin.

> *"And when he is come, he will reprove the world of sin, and of righteousness, and of judgment."*
> *John 16:8*

Without the work and ministry of the Holy Spirit, no person can come to Christ. In Romans 8, the Apostle Paul writes an entire chapter on the subject of **REGENERATION**. To REGENERATE means to be spiritually reborn. It means to be renewed or restored. The dictionary states: **"to form or bring into existence again; re-establish on a new basis."** To be REGENERATED is to be formed again or to be made anew. Such words as "born again," "to be saved," "to receive Christ," "to become a Christian," and "to receive Christ as Saviour" are all terms that we use to describe REGENERATION.

The Apostle Paul writes the entire 8th chapter of Romans to explain the doctrinal truth of REGENERATION. The purpose of REGENERATION is to provide life (eternal life) to the believer. When the believer invites Jesus Christ into his heart, the Holy Spirit comes as the "Spirit of Life."

> *"For the law of the Spirit of life in Christ Jesus hath made me free from the law of sin and death."*
> *Romans 8:2*

The Scripture states that we have life when the Holy Spirit comes as the Spirit of Christ to dwell in us.

"And if Christ be in you, the body is dead because of sin; but the Spirit is life because of righteousness."

Romans 8:10

It is the Holy Spirit who assures us of resurrection from the dead. The Scriptures state,

"But if the Spirit of him that raised up Jesus from the dead dwell in you, he that raised up Christ from the dead shall also give life to your mortal bodies by his Spirit that dwelleth in you."

Romans 8:11

Every person who has confessed his sin and has publicly acknowledged Jesus Christ as Saviour and has asked for forgiveness has received the Holy Spirit. The Holy Spirit enters into us as the "Spirit of Christ." He is also the Spirit of God (Romans 8:9 and Romans 8:14).

EVERY BELIEVER HAS RECEIVED THE HOLY SPIRIT!!

It is impossible to be a Christian without the abiding presence of God's Spirit in our lives.

It is the Holy Spirit that bears witness with our spirit that we are the children of God. This inner witness is the "blessed assurance" that we have been born again. Believers are made anew. We are RE-GENERATED! Christians have eternal life. The Holy

Spirit indwells all believers so that each one can be led and directed by Him.

> *"For as many as are led by the Spirit of God, they are the sons of God."*
>
> *Romans 8:14*

Jesus stated that the Holy Spirit will guide us into all truth....

> *"Howbeit when he, the Spirit of truth, is come, he will guide you into all truth: for he shall not speak of himself; but whatsoever he shall hear, that shall he speak: and he will show you things to come."*
>
> *John 16:13*

> *"Even the Spirit of truth; whom the world cannot receive, because it seeth him not, neither knoweth him: but ye know him; for he dwelleth with you, and shall be in you."*
>
> *John 14:17*

The believer is not left alone. Jesus has sent the blessed Holy Spirit so that we would not be left comfortless. He comes to bear witness that we are, indeed, a child of God.

> *"And I will pray the Father, and he shall give you another Comforter, that he may abide with you forever."*
>
> *John 14:16*

"I will not leave you comfortless; I will come to you."

John 14:18

The Apostle Paul makes it very, very clear that it is impossible to be a Christian without the Holy Spirit indwelling us. We are the temples of God. As we read through this wonderful eighth chapter of Romans, we discover the Holy Spirit is called:

(1) **THE SPIRIT OF LIFE,** verse 2;

"For the law of the <u>Spirit of life</u> in Christ Jesus hath made me free from the law of sin and death."

(2) **THE SPIRIT,** verses 4, 5, 9, 26, and 27;

"...law might be fulfilled in us, who walk not after the flesh, but after <u>the Spirit.</u>"

(Romans 8:4)

"...but they that are after the Spirit the things of <u>the Spirit.</u>"

(Romans 8:5)

"But ye are not in the flesh, but in <u>the Spirit.</u>..."

(Romans 8:9)

"...but <u>the Spirit</u> itself maketh intercession for us with groanings which cannot be uttered."

(Romans 8:26)

5

"And he that searcheth the hearts knoweth what is the mind of the Spirit...."
(Romans 8:27)

(3) **THE SPIRIT OF GOD,** verses 9 and 14;

"For as many as are led by the Spirit of God, they are the sons of God."
Romans 8:14

(4) **THE SPIRIT OF CHRIST,** verse 9;

(5) **THE SPIRIT OF ADOPTION;**

"...but ye have received the Spirit of adoption, whereby we cry, Abba, Father."
Romans 8:15

(6) **THE SPIRIT HIMSELF;**

"The Spirit HIMSELF beareth witness with our spirit, that we are the children of God."
Romans 8:16

"...but the Spirit HIMSELF maketh intercession for us with groanings...."
Romans 8:26

When we receive Jesus Christ as our Saviour, we have His life...eternal life. When we receive Jesus Christ into our hearts, He gives us a spiritual mind and a spiritual understanding.

"For they that are after the flesh do mind the things of the flesh; but they that are after the Spirit the things of the Spirit."

Romans 8:5

"For to be carnally minded is death; but to be spiritually minded is life and peace."
Romans 8:6

"Because the carnal mind is enmity against God: for it is not subject to the law of God, neither indeed can be."

Romans 8:7

In I Corinthians 2:14-16, we learn that the natural man cannot receive the things of God. We have received the Spirit of God, that we might know the things that are freely given to us of God. Paul says:

"Which things also we speak, not in the words which man's wisdom teacheth, but which the Holy Ghost teacheth; comparing spiritual things with spiritual."
I Corinthians 2:13

The carnal mind does not grasp spiritual truth. Our natural minds are at enmity against God and cannot be subject to the law of God. A Christian understands spiritual truths. The Word of God becomes meat and food. The Scriptures are alive. Preaching the Word produces life and power. The Word of God produces and strengthens faith. Without the ministry and work of the Holy Spirit, none of this is possible.

The Holy Spirit has come to do no less than **seven** things:

(1) <u>**THE HOLY SPIRIT IS THE POWER THAT RAISED JESUS FROM THE DEAD**</u> and assures us that we, too, will be resurrected and that our mortal bodies will be raised from the dead.

(2) <u>**THE HOLY SPIRIT GIVES POWER TO MORTIFY OR TO PUT TO DEATH THE DEEDS OF THE BODY.**</u>
Death works in the flesh but God's Spirit gives life to the inner man. We must therefore live after the Spirit.

"If we live in the Spirit, let us also walk in the Spirit."
Galatians 5:25

"For the law of the Spirit of life in Christ Jesus hath made me free from the law of sin and death."
Romans 8:2

(3) <u>**THE HOLY SPIRITS GUIDES THE CHRISTIAN.**</u>
We have a Leader. The Lord has promised to direct our steps. He is the Master and must be Lord in all areas of our lives. The Holy Spirit

is always with us and wants to take control of every step we take.

"...he, the Spirit of truth, is come, he will guide you into all truth: for he shall not speak of himself; but whatsoever he shall hear, that shall he speak: and he will show you things to come."

John 16:13

(4) THE HOLY SPIRIT SETS US FREE FROM THE BONDAGE OF FEAR.

Where the Spirit of God is, there is freedom and deliverance and health and strength. He sets us free. We are not bound.

"For ye have not received the spirit of bondage again to fear; but ye have received the Spirit of adoption, whereby we cry, Abba, Father."

Romans 8:15

Fear brings torment into our lives. Faith is produced by holiness and fear is produced by deception. If we do not permit the Holy Spirit to reign in our life, we will struggle with fear. Some have a fear of death. Others fear the future. We can be tormented by financial fears, physical fears, or fear concerning our future.

Jesus sent the Holy Spirit to dispel fear. We can be set free from *"bondage again to fear"* (Romans 8:15). If you are fearful now, if you are being tormented and brought under bondage because of this binding spirit, the Holy Spirit will deliver you. He was sent to set us free.

(5) **THE SPIRIT OF GOD HAS BROUGHT US INTO AN INTIMATE RELATIONSHIP WITH GOD.**

God is our Father. Jesus Christ is our elder brother. We are an heir of God and joint heir with Christ.

"The Spirit himself beareth witness with our spirit, that we are the children of God:

"And if children, then heirs; heirs of God, and joint-heirs with Christ; if so be that we suffer with him, that we may be also glorified together."

Romans 8:16-17

The Holy Spirit places us in such an intimate relationship with God that we know Him as our Father. We have a blood relationship. We belong to the family of God. The Holy Spirit has made us **"partakers of divine nature."** We are **"the children of God."** The Holy Spirit has provided an intimacy and a new relationship. We are reborn. We have been made anew. We have received the **"Spirit of adoption whereby we cry, Abba, Father."**

(6) **THE HOLY SPIRIT GIVES THE HUMAN SPIRIT A WITNESS, A TESTIMONY, AND AN ASSURANCE.**

We know we have passed from death into life. There are no doubts concerning our relationship with God. The Holy Spirit gives a powerful witness that Jesus Christ is our Saviour, that the Holy Spirit indwells us, and God is our heavenly Father.

"The Spirit HIMSELF beareth witness with our spirit, that we are the children of God."
Romans 8:16

"Hereby know ye the Spirit of God: Every spirit that confesseth that Jesus Christ is come in the flesh is of God."
I John 4:2

"These things have I written unto you that believe on the name of the Son of God; that ye may know that ye have eternal life, and that ye may believe on the name of the Son of God."
I John 5:13

"And we know that the Son of God is come, and hath given us an understanding, that we may know him that is true, and we are in him that is true, even in his Son Jesus Christ. This is the true God, and eternal life."
I John 5:20

(7) <u>**THE HOLY SPIRIT IS A PRAYING SPIRIT.**</u> He helps our weaknesses. **"The Holy Spirit himself maketh intercession"** for us. When we do not know how to pray, the Holy Spirit knows the mind of God. "He maketh interces-

11

sion for the saints according to the will of God."
There is a new dimension to prayer.

"Likewise the Spirit also helpeth our infirmities: for we know not what we should pray for as we ought: but the Spirit HIMSELF maketh intercession for us with groanings which cannot be uttered.

"And he that searcheth the hearts knoweth what is the mind of the Spirit, because he maketh intercession for the saints according to the will of God."
Romans 8:26-27

The Holy Spirit has been sent to us by the Father so that every believer can be **REGENERATED** ("**born again,**" **made anew**) **and receive eternal life.**

"And this is the confidence that we have in him, that, if we ask any thing according to his will, he heareth us:

"And if we know that he hear us, whatsoever we ask, we know that we have the petitions that we desired of him."
I John 5:14-15

There is a danger in some full-gospel, Pentecostal, and charismatic circles to bring confusion into the "Body of Christ" by inferring that people have not received the Holy Spirit until they have been baptized in the Holy Spirit.

There are others who teach that a person is not **REGENERATED** or **SAVED** until they have received the Baptism in the Holy Spirit. These people are often guilty of saying, "You have not received the Holy Spirit until you have been baptized in the Holy Spirit and have experienced speaking in 'an unknown tongue.' "

It is extremely important that all of us recognize that every believer who has asked Jesus Christ to be their Saviour, that has confessed and repented of their sin, and has followed the Lord into the waters of baptism has received the Holy Spirit.

The Apostle Paul stated in I Corinthians 6:19-20 that our bodies are the temples of the Holy Spirit, and He has come to indwell our hearts. A believer may not know anything about the experience of the Baptism in the Holy Spirit. They may not understand **"speaking with other tongues,"** and they may even resist the experience; and still have the Holy Spirit indwelling them.

> *"For as the body is one, and hath many members, and all the members of that one body, being many, are one body: so also is Christ.*
>
> *"For by one Spirit are we all baptized into one body, whether we be Jews or Gentiles, whether we be bond or free; and have been all made to drink into one Spirit.*
>
> *"For the body is not one member, but many."*
>
> *I Corinthians 12:12-14*

We read that there are several baptisms mentioned in the Scripture. However, there are three that are critically important in our relationship with the Lord:

(1) **THE BAPTISM INTO THE "BODY OF CHRIST."**

There is the work and ministry of the Holy Spirit to baptize us into Jesus Christ. The "Body of Christ" has many members but there is only one body. It is the Holy Spirit that makes believers members of this wonderful body. It is the Holy Spirit that places every believer into the "Body of Christ."

(2) **THE BAPTISM IN WATER.**

The GREAT COMMISSION given by our Lord was that the gospel should be preached and that believers must be "baptized in the Name of the Father, and of the Son, and of the Holy Spirit."

"Go ye, therefore, and teach all nations, baptizing them in the name of the Father, and of the Son, and of the Holy Ghost."
Matthew 28:19

The early church followed the instruction and laid down the pattern. Water baptism is not an option! It is a command!

"Then they that gladly received his word were baptized: and the same day there were added unto them about three thousand souls."
Acts 2:41

14

Water baptism is an expression of faith. It is an act of obedience. It is a witness of a work of grace that is done in the heart of a believer; and it is identifying with the death, burial, and resurrection of Jesus Christ. We are buried with Christ and are raised to walk in newness of life. Baptism in water is a deeply spiritual and moving experience for the believer.

(3) **THE BAPTISM IN THE HOLY SPIRIT.**
Jesus spoke concerning this baptism. John was called upon to baptize Jesus in the waters of the Jordan but it is Jesus who baptizes believers into the Holy Spirit. This wonderful baptism is a glorious experience that is provided for everyone who has received the Holy Spirit into their hearts and know that they are a new creature in Christ.

"I indeed baptize you with water unto repentance: but he that cometh after me is mightier than I, whose shoes I am not worthy to bear; he shall baptize you with the Holy Ghost, and with fire."
Matthew 3:11

"And when the day of Pentecost was fully come, they were all with one accord in one place.

"And suddenly there came a sound from heaven as of a rushing mighty wind, and it filled all the house where they were sitting.

15

"And there appeared unto them cloven tongues like as of fire, and it sat upon each of them.

"And they were all filled with the Holy Ghost, and began to speak with other tongues, as the Spirit gave them utterance."

Acts 2:1-4

See also Acts 8:13-19, Acts 10:44-48, and Acts 19:1-7. The entire 8th chapter of Romans is an exposition of the Holy Spirit in REGENERATION. The BAPTISM IN THE HOLY SPIRIT is not mentioned in this chapter. To be REGENERATED is to receive life. The purpose of the Holy Spirit in the work of being **"born again"** is to assure every believer of this life. *REGENERATION IS FOR THE PURPOSE OF LIFE!*

CHAPTER 2

THE WORK OF THE HOLY SPIRIT IN INFILLING

The Holy Spirit was given to fill every believer. In Ephesians 5:18-21, we read the following words:

> *"And be not drunk with wine, wherein is excess; but* **BE FILLED WITH THE SPIRIT."**

On the day of Pentecost, believers were filled with the Holy Spirit (Acts 2:1-4).

> *"And they were all filled with the Holy Ghost, and began to speak with other tongues, as the Spirit gave them utterance."*
>
> *Acts 2:4*

The early church sought the Lord when Peter and John were thrust into prison, and it is recorded that those who were assembled together were all filled with the Holy Spirit.

"And when they had prayed, the place was shaken where they were assembled together; and they were all filled with the Holy Ghost, and they spoke the word of God with boldness."

Acts 4:31

To the proportion that a believer is filled with the Spirit, he portrays the character and nature of Jesus Christ. The Apostle Paul said that the "fruit of the Spirit" (love, joy, peace, long-suffering, gentleness, goodness, faith, meekness, temperance) will be manifested in the life of a Christian to the degree that a Christian is filled with the Spirit of God. Christian character is produced by the Spirit of the Lord.

The Apostle Paul makes a contrast between the "works of the flesh" and "the fruit of the Spirit." We are admonished to walk in the Spirit so we will not fulfill the lust of the flesh.

"But the fruit of the Spirit is love, joy, peace, long-suffering, gentleness, goodness, faith,

"Meekness, temperance: against such there is no law.

"And they that are Christ's have crucified the flesh with the affections and lusts.

"If we live in the Spirit, let us also walk in the Spirit.

"Let us not be desirous of vain-glory, provoking one another, envying one another."
Acts 5:22-26

A Christian will not walk after the flesh if he is filled with the Spirit.

"For the flesh lusteth against the Spirit, and the Spirit against the flesh; and these are contrary the one to the other: so that ye cannot do the things that ye would.

"But if ye be led of the Spirit, ye are not under the law."
Galatians 5:17-18

It is possible for a Christian to be filled with the Spirit when he has not ever received the experience of the Baptism in the Holy Spirit. This is the reason that there are committed and spiritual Christians with beautiful Christian character who have never spoken with tongues and have never received their spiritual baptism.

This is also the reason that there are those who have received a spiritual baptism and still rejoice in the blessing, glory, power, and emotion of the experience but do not demonstrate the **"fruit of the Spirit."**

A Christian can be baptized in the Spirit and not be filled with the Spirit; and, a Christian can be filled

19

with the Spirit and never experience the Baptism in the Spirit.

The baptism in the Holy Spirit is a <u>GLORIOUS SPIRITUAL EXPERIENCE.</u> Being filled with the Spirit is an <u>ONGOING RELATIONSHIP.</u> A Spirit-filled Christian has joy. A Spirit-filled Christian possesses peace. A Spirit-filled Christian expresses the love of God in his relationship with others. The "fruit of the Spirit" is produced as the Person of the Holy Spirit fills and controls the life of a believer. There is ONE SPIRITUAL BAPTISM! There are MANY IN-FILLINGS!

The Apostle Paul addressed this difference when he wrote the 13th chapter of I Corinthians, verse 1. He stated that

> *"Though I speak with the tongues of men and of angels, and have not love, I am become as sounding brass, or tinkling cymbal."*

He clearly states that it is possible for one of the spirituals to function in the life of a believer and yet, that believer not have the "fruit of the Spirit" in their life. A spiritual experience without Christian character produces damaging results. All too often, individuals who have been wonderfully baptized in the Holy Spirit become so enthralled with the experience that they do not seek the Lord that they would be filled with the Spirit on a day-to-day basis.

A Spirit-filled believer will be filled with psalms and hymns, and spiritual songs. He will sing and make melody in his heart to the Lord. A Spirit-filled Christian will give thanks unto God in the Name of

20

the Lord Jesus Christ. He will be filled with gratitude. A Spirit-filled Christian will possess an attitude of submission. They will submit one to another. The husband will submit to the Lord. The wife will submit to the husband. A Spirit-filled Christian will be Christlike.

> *"And be not drunk with wine, wherein is excess; but be filled with the Spirit;*
>
> *"Speaking to yourselves in psalms and hymns and spiritual songs, singing and making melody in your heart to the Lord;*
>
> *"Giving thanks always for all things unto God and the Father in the name of our Lord Jesus Christ;*
>
> *"Submitting yourselves one to another in the fear of God."*
> *Ephesians 5:18-21*

The Holy Spirit has come to glorify Jesus Christ in our lives. A Spirit-filled Christian will have victory over carnality. The Apostle Paul said:

> *"And I, brethren, could not speak unto you as unto spiritual, but as unto carnal, even as unto babes in Christ."*
> *I Corinthians 3:1*

The person who is filled with the Holy Spirit will speak the Word of God with boldness.

"And when they had prayed, the place was shaken where they were assembled together; and they were all filled with the Holy Ghost, and they spoke the word of God with boldness."

Acts 4:31

The light and life of Christ will shine forth through a Spirit-filled Christian. Spirit-filled Christians will have a good testimony and will be candidates to be used in the service of the Lord. The apostles instructed the church to look for seven men of honest report **"full of the Holy Spirit** that we may appoint them to be deacons." The deacons in the early church were men filled with the Holy Spirit. It is no wonder that the power of God rested upon the believers.

Deacon Stephen was giving his testimony before the Sanhedrin in Jerusalem. As he spoke, those who heard him "were cut to the heart and they gnashed on him with their teeth." The Scripture goes on to say:

"But he, being full of the Holy Ghost, looked up steadfastly into heaven, and saw the glory of God, and Jesus standing on the right hand of God."

Acts 7:55

He cried out to the Lord that the Lord would forgive those who were stoning him. Saul of Tarsus was a witness to the stoning of Stephen and was so affected by the fact that Stephen was **full of the Holy Spirit** that God used it to touch the heart of the persecutor of the church. Paul saw Jesus Christ in the life of Stephen, the deacon.

The greatest need in the "full-gospel" church is that we would move past spiritual experience into an intimate and personal relationship with the Lord. This would remove all pride.

The Holy Spirit has come to dwell in our hearts. He wants us to be filled with His presence and His power. He was sent to glorify Jesus in and through us. We have received the "life of the Spirit" that we may produce the "fruit of the Spirit" and be witnesses of Jesus Christ in our world.

The Holy Spirit's work in **REGENERATION** is to produce life in the believer. The work of the Holy Spirit in the believer is to fill each of us so that the character of Christ can be produced in us and the "fruit of the Spirit" can be manifested through us.

INFILLING PRODUCES CHRISTIAN CHARACTER. Being raised in a Pentecostal church, I have observed hundreds and hundreds of people who have received the Baptism in the Holy Spirit. All too often, there was great rejoicing over this experience but very little evidence of spiritual growth and maturity.

"But the fruit of the Spirit is love, joy, peace, long-suffering, gentleness, goodness, faith,

"Meekness, temperance...."
Galatians 5:22-23

Too many have felt that the "experience" was an end in itself. Some who have received the Baptism in the Holy Spirit no longer have joy. Peace has been taken from them. Fear and frustration control them. Anxiety, resentment, and criticism drive them. A **RE-LATIONSHIP** with the Holy Spirit was not developed.

Christians are temples. We are vessels!! The Holy Spirit wants to fill and control every area of our lives. He wants to control our thought life and direct our steps into righteousness and holiness. The Holy Spirit wants the life of Christ to shine forth through every believer. He wants us to have His joy, His peace, His love, His patience, and His meekness. It is so easy for us to let other things fill our lives.

When we are filled with the Spirit, there is no place for the flesh. When we walk after the Spirit, we will not fulfill the lust of the flesh. Spirit-baptized believers need to be very sensitive and careful about placing so much emphasis on the "experience" if we have not permitted the Person of the Holy Spirit to fill our lives. The world needs **Spirit-filled** believers! Paul's command still rings clear: ***"Be not drunk with wine, wherein is excess, but BE FILLED WITH THE SPIRIT."*** The Holy Spirit is present **TO SAVE US** and **TO FILL US** (Ephesians 5)!

CHAPTER 3

THE WORK OF THE HOLY SPIRIT IN ANOINTING

Jesus said, "The Spirit of the Lord is upon me for he hath ANOINTED me" (Luke 4:18). **REGENERA-TION** by the Holy Spirit produces LIFE! The IN-FILLING of the Holy Spirit produces Christian CHARACTER! The ANOINTING of the Holy Spirit is always for SERVICE!

It is possible that the **ANOINTING** of God's Spirit may be upon a person who does not have Christian character or the "fruit of the spirit." This was the case with Samson. The Spirit of the Lord would come upon him and he would do exploits. Even when his life was inconsistent with Godly principles, the ANOINTING continued to rest upon him for a long period of time.

Some have confused the **"blessing of the Lord"** or **"the inspiration of the Spirit"** with the **"anointing of the Spirit."** Unless we are committed to service, there is no anointing upon us. When Jesus stood in the synagogue and read the Scripture concerning the ANOINTING, He immediately began His public ministry.

"The Spirit of the Lord is upon me, because he hath anointed me to preach the gospel to the poor; he hath sent me to heal the brokenhearted, to preach deliverance to the captives, and recovering of sight to the blind, to set at liberty them that are bruised,

"To preach the acceptable year of the Lord."
Luke 4:18-19

Jesus was born of the Spirit, and as He entered into His earthly ministry, the ANOINTING of God's Spirit rested heavily upon Him.

As a young man raised in the parsonage of a Pentecostal preacher, I would on occasions see ministries that God was using where their lives did not measure up to Godly standards and principles. This often troubled me because I felt that an **ANOINTING** upon a ministry was always a guarantee that the ministry was conducting itself in righteousness and Godliness.

It was a revelation to me to learn that the ANOINTING often rests upon vessels who are immature, inconsistent, and even unholy. Sooner or later, God deals with these defects; but, in the process, His power and ANOINTING will continue to rest upon that person.

In Exodus 30, we are given a divine order of things. In verses 11-16, provision is made for God's people in redemption. Then, in verses 17-21, the Lord spoke to Moses and instructed him to make "a laver of bronze." This was so the redeemed people of God could know the cleansing power of God.

"Let us draw near with a true heart in full assurance of faith, having our hearts sprinkled from an evil conscience, and our bodies washed with pure water."
Hebrews 10:22

"If we confess our sins, he is faithful and just to forgive us our sins, and to cleanse us from all unrighteousness."
I John 1:9

God continues to speak to Moses in Exodus 30:22-23 concerning THE HOLY ANOINTING OIL. After redemption and after cleansing, ANOINTING was available. God said in verse 30: **"And thou shalt ANOINT Aaron and his sons, and consecrate them, THAT THEY MAY MINISTER UNTO ME IN THE PRIEST'S OFFICE."**

The ANOINTING oil was placed upon the priest in order for him to minister in the priest's office. The ANOINTING oil was never to be placed on a stranger. The only things that were to be ANOINTED were those vessels, instruments, and persons that would SERVE the Lord in ministry. The ANOINTING was for SERVICE!

INSPIRATION VERSUS ANOINTING

There is a difference between INSPIRATION and ANOINTING. Inspiration is an emotional experience! It is a stimulus to our thoughts and our actions. It prompts an emotional response. Ministries can be inspired by the reaction of the crowd or by the size of the crowd. They can become excited and emotional over the content of their message.

Inspiration can be produced when a speaker is gifted in stirring and moving an audience. The beat or the rhythm of music can inspire. The intonation and the content of a sermon can produce inspiration. The mood and the reaction of the people can be an inspiring experience. However, all of this can be present without the ANOINTING of the Spirit of God.

It is easy to experience "inspiration" in the secular world. The comedian experiences it. The actor on the stage knows well what it means to be inspired. The athlete on the playing field can perform with exciting inspiration and can accomplish a great deal under the power and strength of it.

The Holy Spirit is the only one that can ANOINT. This ANOINTING rests upon a person when the commitment to service is made.

BLESSING VERSUS ANOINTING

The "blessing of the Lord" is oftentimes misunderstood as the ANOINTING. The Spirit of the Lord moves upon us and we feel great joy. The power of God comes into our lives and produces deliverance.

We are set free from some bondage or fear! The believer is released from some burden or torment. The heart rejoices!! We are filled with gratitude and suddenly, we break forth in praise, adulation, and worship.

The feeling is ecstatic!!! The release that is felt is indescribable. On occasions such as this, many lift their hands in thanksgiving to God. Others clap their hands in praise and worship to the Lord. It is not uncommon to see people dance, sing, weep, shout, and express great exuberance because of the blessing of God. However, there is a difference between **BLESSING** and the **ANOINTING** of the Spirit of God!

After pastoring for more than fifty years, I have watched people come to church who would respond to ministry because they were seeking a blessing. If a singer could come that would stir their emotions, or if a preacher was a gifted communicator and could inspire and stir with their ministry, people were blessed. I have watched over the years as people have sought the Lord and followed ministry **because they were interested in the blessing!**

If someone could bless them, if someone could stir their emotion, if someone could inspire them, they would return home lifted in their spirit and anxious to return for another blessing. I have heard thousands of people seek the Lord for His blessing. The prayer that has been heard at our altars over the years has been **"Oh, Lord, bless me and my house."**

Thank God for His blessing! It is wonderful when the Lord stirs our emotion. It is exciting to be blessed of the Lord. The wise man said in Proverbs 10:22:

"**The blessing of the Lord maketh rich.**" In Proverbs 28:20, the Scripture tells us that "**A faithful man shall abound with blessing.**" The prophet Malachi warned the children of Israel that God would curse their blessing; but He promised God's people if they would be faithful with their tithe and their offerings that He would pour out a blessing that they could not contain.

> *"Bring ye all the tithes into the storehouse, that there may be meat in mine house, and prove now herewith, saith the Lord of hosts, if I will not open you the windows of heaven, and pour you out a blessing, that there shall not be room enough to receive it."*
> *Malachi 3:10*

The Lord wants His people to be blessed! He wants to bless us physically and He wants to bless us financially. He wants to bless our families and our homes. He wants to bless His people in the market place. He wants to bless our children. The Lord delights to bless His people and certainly His blessings abound. The Lord can turn a curse into blessing.

> *"...but the Lord thy God turned the curse into a blessing unto thee, because the Lord thy God loved thee."*
> *Deuteronomy 23:5b*

God's blessing should produce worship. The blessings call us to break forth with singing and with laughter. The blessing of the Lord will cause the children of God to offer praise. There is a little chorus that is often sung in our churches:

"I am blessed, I am blessed, Every day of my life I am blessed."

This is the testimony of God's people. The Lord pours His blessings upon us and we thank God for them.

God said to Abraham:

"Surely blessing I will bless thee...."
                                        Hebrews 6:14a

Peter admonishes the saints not to:

"render evil for evil, or railing for railing: but contrariwise blessing; knowing that ye are thereunto called, that ye should inherit a blessing."
                                              I Peter 3:9

The Apostle Paul wrote that God

"hath blessed us with all spiritual blessing in heavenly places in Christ."
                                        Ephesians 1:3

The Holy Spirit brings great blessing into our lives. As I reflect back over years of ministry, I can count hundreds of times when the blessing of the Lord rested upon me. He blessed me when I was not filled with the Spirit. He blessed me when I was disobedient and unfaithful. He blessed me when I was not committed to service. The Holy Spirit is loving, patient, and desires to bless God's people. **He is the Blesser!**

Too often many that have been the recipients of such blessing have done very little in faithful service to the Lord. One of the disconcerting things that I have noticed in my ministry is that, oftentimes, people who have been blessed with great talent and financial ability have not been faithful, dependable, committed, or loyal to the work of the ministry. Money can be given, but faithfulness to the church can be lacking.

I have observed that all too often, those who can respond so quickly with their emotions cannot be depended upon to carry a load. When you ask them to serve, they have excuses to offer and will hedge against a commitment. If some are not blessed, if they can't be lifted to a "spiritual high," if difficulties come to the "body" and a battle ensues in spiritual matters, those who depend upon blessing search for another source. I have watched, in dismay, people who came and shouted when we shouted, sang when we sang, rejoiced when we rejoiced, but forsook the "Body" when reverses came and the church would face hard times.

Those who live for blessing only are usually shallow and fade as the flowers. The Holy Spirit is the Blesser. He delights in blessing all of us. **REGENERATION PRODUCES LIFE.** The **INFILLING PRODUCES FRUIT AND CHARACTER.** The **ANOINTING PROVIDES ABILITY FOR US TO SERVE AND TO MINISTER;** and the **BLESSING GENERATES PRAISE, WORSHIP,** and a **SPIRIT**

OF GRATITUDE AND THANKSGIVING. These are the works of the Holy Spirit!

CHAPTER 4

THE WORK OF THE HOLY SPIRIT IN BAPTISM

There are many questions that need responses:

(1) Has every believer received the Holy Spirit?

(2) Is the BAPTISM IN THE HOLY SPIRIT and the baptism spoken of by the Apostle Paul in I Corinthians the same?

> *"For by one Spirit are we all baptized into one body, whether we be Jews or Gentiles, whether we be bond or free; and have been all made to drink into one Spirit.*
>
> *"For the body is not one member, but many."*
>
> *I Corinthians 12:13-14*

(3) Can the "spirituals" (gifts of the Spirit) function and operate through a person who has not received the BAPTISM IN THE HOLY SPIRIT?

(4) Does everyone who has received the BAPTISM IN THE HOLY SPIRIT speak with other tongues (unknown tongues)?

(5) Is the BAPTISM IN THE HOLY SPIRIT for us today?

(6) Is the BAPTISM IN THE HOLY SPIRIT and sanctification the same thing?

(7) Is it possible to be sanctified and not have received the BAPTISM IN THE HOLY SPIRIT and be living a sanctified life?

Since I was born into a PENTECOSTAL home, I have been exposed an entire lifetime to "the Pentecostal movement." I have witnessed thousands of people experience the BAPTISM IN THE HOLY SPIRIT! I have averaged more than five hundred church services a year for the past fifty years in Pentecostal, full gospel, and charismatic churches.

Often there have been confusion and excesses. Misunderstanding has resulted because of semantics. One expression or term has been used that means one thing to one person and something different to another. The "experience" has ofttimes been emphasized over relationship. Spiritual gifts have been coveted more than a godly life. Blessing has been prioritized over service!

In spite of these weaknesses, the number of "Spirit baptized" people is now into the millions. During the "CHARISMATIC MOVEMENT," the Lord Jesus Christ baptized believers in the historic churches. Multiplied thousands sought the Lord and received their spiritual baptism. Catholics, Presbyterians, Lutherans, Episcopalians, Baptists, and others sought the Lord and received the BAPTISM IN THE HOLY SPIRIT.

A new liberty of worship resulted. Singing, rejoicing, dancing, and praising characterized those who were so enriched by the "experience." Speaking in other tongues was no longer discarded, mocked, or rejected. People in all walks of life realized that there was a spiritual experience that could move believers into a deeper and broader relationship with the Lord Jesus than they had ever known. There has been a spiritual renewal! The Lord has blessed His people with an awakening!! The words of the prophet Joel have a ring of reality today. (See also Acts 2:14-21.)

"And it shall come to pass afterward, that I will pour out my spirit upon all flesh; and your sons and your daughters shall prophesy, your old men shall dream dreams, your young men shall see visions:

"And also upon servants and upon the handmaids in those days will I pour out my spirit."
Joel 2:28-29

First, I would like to address the subject:

WHAT IS THE BAPTISM IN THE HOLY SPIRIT?

When a believer is baptized in water, it is the minister who does the baptizing. It is the believer who is baptized, and the element into which he is baptized is water!

When a person receives Jesus Christ as his personal Saviour, he becomes a member of the Body of Christ. The Apostle Paul makes this clear in I Corinthians:

"For as the body is one, and hath many members, and all the members of that one body, being many, are one body: so also is Christ."
I Corinthians 12:12

Every believer in the Lord Jesus Christ is a member of the Body of Christ. No church, denomination, or group has exclusive rights to this privilege. Every person, regardless of color, age, or culture, can be a member of the Lord's Body. The moment a person receives Christ as his Saviour, the Holy Spirit baptizes them into the Body of Christ (**I Corinthians 12:13-14**).

Without this baptism, no one is a member of the Body. EVERYONE who comes to Christ is made a member of the Body of Christ by this baptism. At that moment, we are set into the Body of Christ and become "members in particular."

"Now ye are the body of Christ, and members in particular."
I Corinthians 12:27

It is important that all Christians understand that this baptism places all of us into Christ. Christ has only one Body. He is the Head of one church. There are hundreds of denominations but only one church. There are millions of believers but only one Body.

"For as the body is one, and hath many members, and all the members of that one body, being many, are one body: so also is Christ."
I Corinthians 12:12

It is time that everyone who names Jesus Christ as Saviour recognizes that we are brothers and sisters and members of the same family. If we would walk in the light of this truth, there would be a unity among believers. The things that separate and divide us would be minimized and we could fellowship together as one in Christ. We may differ in many doctrinal insights, but it is time that GOD'S PEOPLE recognize one another as "partakers of divine nature."

There is a baptism into water, and there is baptism into the Body of Christ. When John spoke concerning baptism, he said that there was one coming who would have a different baptism.

"I indeed baptize you with water unto repentance: but he that cometh after me is

mightier than I, whose shoes I am not worthy to bear: he shall baptize you with the Holy Ghost, and with fire:

"Whose fan is in his hand, and he will thoroughly purge his floor, and gather his wheat into the garner; but he will burn up the chaff with unquenchable fire."
Matthew 3:11-12

John was speaking of the baptism with the Holy Spirit. On the day of Pentecost, several things happened simultaneously to those believers:

(1) The Person of the Holy Spirit came to indwell every believer and to draw people to Christ.

(2) Every person that was in the upper room was FILLED with the Holy Spirit (Acts 2:4).

(3) They were BLESSED by the Holy Spirit.

(4) They were ANOINTED to speak forth the wonderful news of God.

(5) Peter was ANOINTED to stand and proclaim the gospel of Jesus Christ.

(6) They all were BAPTIZED IN THE HOLY SPIRIT.

This is made clear because evidence of the experience was that each believer spoke with "tongues." This special "evidence" was present at the household of Cornelius.

"While Peter yet spake these words, the Holy Ghost fell on all them which heard the word.

"And they of the circumcision which believed were astonished...."

Acts 10:45-46

Under the Apostle Paul's ministry, they spoke "with tongues" when the Holy Spirit came on them.

"And when Paul had laid his hands upon them, the Holy Ghost came on them; and they spake with tongues, and prophesied."

Acts 19:6

In water baptism, our bodies are placed in the water.

In the BAPTISM IN THE HOLY SPIRIT, it is the "human spirit" that is baptized. In salvation, the first physical evidence of the experience is "confession with the mouth." A person can believe in their heart that Jesus is the Saviour but they must bear witness with their mouth and declare Christ to be Lord and Saviour. Then, the believer is filled with joy and possesses a blessed assurance.

When the believer's spirit is baptized, the human spirit will speak forth a witness to this baptism. An English speaking person, when speaking in English, speaks with the mind and the understanding. But when the spirit of a believer speaks, the mouth will speak words that the mind does not comprehend or understand. The Apostle Paul declares:

"For if I pray in an unknown tongue, my spirit prayeth, but my understanding is unfruitful.

41

"What is it then? I will pray with the spirit, and I will pray with the under-standing also: I will sing with the spirit, and I will sing with the understanding also."

I Corinthians 14:14-15

He makes a distinction between speaking with the "understanding" and speaking with the "spirit." Only a baptized spirit can speak in "tongues." The speaking with "tongues" is not the only evidence of a spiritual baptism, but it is the first physical evidence!! In each case where the Holy Spirit came upon believers, it was evidenced by their speaking with "tongues."

There is a distinction made in being baptized into the Body of Christ and being baptized "with the Holy Spirit." Jesus brings the believer into this experience. Jesus is the Saviour, the BAPTIZER, the Healer, and He is the soon-coming King.

HOW TO RECEIVE THE HOLY SPIRIT

There is no set formula for a person receiving this experience. It is almost pointless to write guidelines for experiencing the Baptism in the Holy Spirit. It is Jesus who does the baptizing. It is necessary that we come to Him for this glorious experience.

However, there are some very important steps that must be taken **BEFORE** this is possible. There are some steps that need to be taken in order that we may become candidates for this baptism.

FIRST, A PERSON MUST BE BORN AGAIN. Without repentance and confession of Jesus Christ as

Saviour, there can never be a spiritual baptism. A person cannot qualify because they are a member of a church, or because they have lived a good life. Doing good deeds and being a proper person is not sufficient to receive the **BAPTISM IN THE HOLY SPIRIT.**

Then, we receive the **BAPTISM IN THE HOLY SPIRIT** when we ask Jesus for it.

> *"And I say unto you, Ask, and it shall be given you; seek, and ye shall find; knock, and it shall be opened unto you."*
> *Luke 11:9*

There are instances where people have received the baptism without asking for it. In Acts 10:44, we read that the people who had gathered in the home of Cornelius were gloriously baptized and they all spoke with "tongues." This is an exception to the rule.

Asking Jesus for anything is an expression of faith! The Lord honors us when we come to Him trusting His promises.

Then, we receive the baptism when we are willing to believe that we have received. In the spiritual walk, seeing is not believing. The very opposite is true. Believing is seeing.

> *" ...That whosoever shall say unto this mountain, be thou removed, and be thou cast into the sea; and shall not doubt in his heart, but shall believe that those things which he saith shall come to pass; he shall have whatsoever he saith.*

"Therefore I say unto you, What things soever ye desire; when ye pray, believe that ye receive them, and ye shall have them."
Mark 11:23-24

In conversion, we must believe in our heart that Jesus Christ died, was buried and rose again. We must acknowledge that He is our living Saviour. Then, it is necessary for us to give an expression of our faith. We must confess with our mouth that we believe in our heart.

The disciples received the baptism through the laying on of hands. Today thousands of people experience this glorious baptism when hands are laid on them in the Name of the Lord (Acts 19:6).

In every case in the Scripture, where it is evident that persons receive the BAPTISM IN THE HOLY SPIRIT, they speak in tongues. Peter knew that Cornelius and his household had received the baptism for they heard them speak with tongues.

There must also be an expression of faith. Without the believer yielding his life, his voice, his will, and his mind to the Lord, there will be no baptism. When an attitude of worship and praise fills the heart and we surrender totally to the Lord, He will baptize us. The Lord does the baptizing, but we must do the speaking.

As long as we speak in our native language, our spirit is not totally yielded to the Lord. When we begin to speak words that have no meaning or significance to our mind, it gives our renewed spirit the privilege of praying and praising in a dimension the believer has never experienced before.

We need not be fearful or hesitant when we ask the Lord to baptize us.

"If a son shall ask bread of any of you that is a father, will he give him a stone? or if he ask for a fish, will he for a fish give him a serpent?

"Or if he shall ask an egg, will he offer him a scorpion?

"If ye then, being evil, know how to give good gifts unto your children: how much more shall your heavenly Father give the Holy Spirit to them that ask him?"
Luke 11:11-13

So we need to distinguish between the work of the Holy Spirit in REGENERATION, ANOINTING, IN-FILLING, and BAPTISM. In REGENERATION, we are "born again." We receive spiritual life. We are quickened and made alive by the Spirit that raised Jesus from the dead.

"And you hath he quickened, who were dead in trespasses and sins;

"Wherein in time past ye walked according to the course of this world, according to the prince of the power of the air, the spirit that now worketh in the children of disobedience:

"Among whom also we all had our conversation in times past in the lusts of our

45

flesh, fulfilling the desires of the flesh and of the mind; and were by nature the children of wrath, even as others.

"But God, who is rich in mercy, for his great love wherewith he loved us,

"Even when we were dead in sins, hath quickened us together with Christ (by grace ye are saved)."
                                    Ephesians 2:1-5

When the Holy Spirit ANOINTS us, it is because we have committed ourselves to serve the Lord someplace in His church. His ANOINTING empowers us to do the work of the ministry.

Then, the Holy Spirit BLESSES us and FILLS us. He BLESSES us in order to encourage praise and worship. Then, the BAPTISM IN THE HOLY SPIRIT moves the believer into a deeper relationship with the Lord. Prayer life is expanded. There is a new dimension to praise and worship. The BAPTISM IN THE HOLY SPIRIT is the door for the Holy Spirit to manifest Himself through the believer with the "spirituals." Love for the Lord Jesus is intensified and a sensitivity to the will of the Lord is sharpened.

THIS IS THAT!

On the day of Pentecost, the Holy Spirit came to indwell believers. Every believer is a temple for the Holy Spirit. From the time the Father sent the Holy

Spirit, believers have been FILLED, BLESSED, ANOINTED, and BAPTIZED.

When Peter stood up to explain the phenomena, he quoted from the prophet Joel and said:

"And it shall come to pass afterward, that I will pour out my spirit upon all flesh; and your sons and your daughters shall prophesy, your old men shall dream dreams, your young men shall see visions:

"And also upon servants and upon the handmaids in those days will I pour out my spirit."

(Joel 2:28-29)

"THIS IS THAT" was not only PROPHESIED by Joel but was PREDICTED by John the Baptist. John said:

"I indeed baptize you with water unto repentance: but he that cometh after me is mightier than I, whose shoes I am not worthy to bear: he shall baptize you with the Holy Ghost, and with fire."

John 3:11

Peter shared in his sermon that the Holy Spirit had been given.

"Then Peter said unto them, Repent, and be baptized every one of you in the name of Jesus Christ for the remission of sins, and ye shall receive the gift of the Holy Ghost."

Acts 2:38

John the Baptist said that this baptism would be a baptism of fire. Fire denotes the presence of God. This baptism was promised by Jesus. Jesus is the Baptizer. In the teaching of Jesus concerning the work of the Holy Spirit in the believer, He describes three distinct phases.

He said the Holy Spirit would be:

(1) *"WITH YOU"...(John 14:17)*.

(2) *"IN YOU"...(John 14:17)*.

(3) *"UPON YOU"...(Luke 24:49)*.

Jesus said He would be "WITH YOU" to guide. He shall "guide you into all truth."

> *"Howbeit when he, the Spirit of truth, is come, he will guide you into all truth: for he shall not speak of himself; but whatsoever he shall hear, that shall he speak: and he will show you things to come."*
> *John 16:13*

He is to be "IN YOU" in REGENERATION. Just as Adam became a living soul in Genesis 2:7, so we become partakers of a divine nature through the Holy Ghost.

The Holy Spirit comes "UPON YOU" to give power. This "power from on high" is to cause every believer to be a witness. The Holy Spirit gives life! The Holy Spirit FILLS, BLESSES, and ANOINTS us. Then, the Scriptures make clear that every believer can be BAPTIZED INTO THE HOLY SPIRIT. The Holy Spirit was predominant in the early church. The church was **SPIRIT FILLED** and **SPIRIT CONTROLLED** (Acts 8:17).

The Holy Spirit was poured out into the lives of those who were gathered in the home of Cornelius (Acts 10:46). Peter testified in Jerusalem that "the Holy Spirit fell on them as on us at the beginning" (Acts 11:15). The criticism of the brethren ceased and praise commenced.

Nearly twenty years after Pentecost, there was a similar outpouring in the city of Ephesus (Acts 19:1-7). It is evident that the **BAPTISM IN THE SPIRIT** was a standard experience among the believers in the early church. Sometimes it was necessary to tarry. Sometimes it happened during the laying on of hands. Sometimes it was a completely spontaneous experience. However, it always came after conversion and was a distinct and separate experience. The glorious Person of the Holy Spirit predominated and empowered the life of the first century church.

The **BAPTISM IN THE SPIRIT** occupied a permanent place in the Apostolic church. There is no indication that it was that generation's exclusive possession. Down through the centuries, men and women of God have enjoyed the same experience that happened to the one hundred twenty believers on the day of Pentecost.

Today people react in various ways to this spiritual phenomenon. Some are amazed. Others are in doubt. Some attempt to explain away the experience. They reject the supernatural. Peter declared that "THIS IS THAT which Joel prophesied." **"THIS IS THAT"** is still happening in the Body of Christ today!

THE INITIAL EVIDENCE

The doctrine that "speaking with other tongues" is the initial evidence of the BAPTISM IN THE HOLY SPIRIT rests upon recorded cases in the Book of Acts. The New Testament contains no plain categorical statement concerning what must be the sign. However, the conclusion is that the initial physical evidence of the BAPTISM IN THE SPIRIT is "speaking with other tongues." It is the result of a logical sequence of reasoning.

The New Testament teaches that the BAPTISM IN THE HOLY SPIRIT is a definite experience. It is not the same as REGENERATION. It is different than the ANOINTING. And the experience is not the same as **SANCTIFICATION.**

This spiritual experience must consist of some outward manifestation. The outward manifestation of the "new birth" experience is a confession by the believer that he has received Christ as Saviour.

As we carefully examine the records mentioned in the Book of Acts, we will immediately conclude that the initial physical evidence of this experience is, indeed, "speaking with tongues."

(1) **THE DAY OF PENTECOST.** It is clear that tongues were the divinely chosen evidence to the outpouring of the Holy Spirit. The early believers received the Person of the Holy Spirit and simultaneously "experienced" the BAPTISM IN THE HOLY SPIRIT. Every believer spoke with "tongues" in this case. It was a supernatural manifestation of the "experience."

(2) **SAMARIA (Acts 8:14-18).** In this particular case, there is no apparent indication as to the nature of the manifestation; however, when we read verses 18 and 19, we must logically conclude that Simon observed something supernatural and made an amazing request.

"And when Simon saw that through laying on of the apostles' hands the Holy Ghost was given, he offered them money,

"Saying, Give me also this power, that on whomsoever I lay hands, he may receive the Holy Ghost."

Acts 8:18-19

This is proof that something very obvious had taken place.

Since the other cases in the Bible indicate that the manifestation of "speaking with tongues" was present, we are certainly justified in believing that this was the case in Samaria. "Speaking with other tongues" meets all of the requirements of the context.

(3) **SAUL OF TARSUS (Acts 9:17; I Corinthians 14:18).** The Scriptures do not record when the Apostle Paul received this experience. When we read Paul's strong personal testimony in I Corinthians 14, we realize that he did speak with "tongues." It was he who wrote three chapters concerning the "spirituals" (commonly referred to as the gifts of the Spirit). There is every reason to believe that Paul received this particular manifestation of "speaking with tongues" at some point in his spiritual experience just

as the other apostles received it when they were baptized in the Holy Spirit.

(4) **THE HOUSEHOLD OF CORNELIUS (Acts 10:44-47).** The Scriptures state conclusively that the evidence that satisfied the Jewish believers that the Gentiles had received the Holy Spirit was their "speaking with tongues." In verse 46 we read, "for they heard them speak with tongues." This is a definite statement concerning this evidence. It reveals that this unique sign had already been accepted in the New Testament church.

(5) **EPHESIAN BELIEVERS (Acts 19:1-6).** This company of twelve men received the Holy Spirit. The Scriptures plainly state: "They spake with tongues and prophesied." Nothing could be more clear! Some nineteen years had passed since the day of Pentecost but the same identical initial evidence is found accompanying the BAPTISM IN THE HOLY SPIRIT.

It is clear that this evidence of "speaking in tongues" is spontaneous (Acts 10:44-46). The gift of "speaking with tongues" is controllable (I Corinthians 14:28). The initial evidence can be given to any number as was done on the day of Pentecost, or a room full of people as at the home of Cornelius, or on twelve as is recorded in Acts 19 concerning those who were at Ephesus.

The use of the gift is limited to "two or at the most three" (I Corinthians 14:27). These passages completely contradict one another unless a distinction is made between "tongues" as an initial evidence of the BAPTISM IN THE HOLY SPIRIT and "tongues" as the "gift" in the Body of Christ.

WHAT MUST BE DONE TO RECEIVE THE BAPTISM IN THE HOLY SPIRIT?

There are several things that a believer can do to position himself so the Lord can baptize him.

(1) **The believer must seek the Lord with all his heart.** Halfhearted seekers will never receive this blessing. The prophet Jeremiah stated:

> *"And ye shall seek me, and find me, when ye shall search for me with all your heart."*
> *Jeremiah 29:13*

God demands unwavering faith when we ask the Lord to do anything for us.

> *"But let him ask in faith, nothing wavering. For he that wavereth is like a wave of the sea driven with the wind and tossed.*
>
> *"For let not that man think that he shall receive any thing of the Lord."*
> *James 1:6-7*

When we combine a strong faith with a deep sense of our need, we have met the necessary prerequisites for receiving this glorious experience.

(2) **We must thirst after a deep relationship with the Lord. God feeds hungry souls.** When a believer feels that his greatest need is to be baptized with the Spirit, then they will receive the divine blessing and be satisfied.

"I stretch forth my hands unto thee: my soul thirsteth after thee, as a thirsty land."
Psalm 143:6

"I have longed for my salvation, 0 Lord; and thy law is my delight."
Psalm 119:174

Do we feel what the Psalmist felt? Is our spirit parched and dry? Do we long for God in the same way that the desert longs for water? He has promised that He would quench our thirst.

"For I will pour water upon him that is thirsty, and floods upon the dry ground: I will pour my spirit upon thy seed, and my blessing upon thine offspring."
Isaiah 44:3

(3) **Our motives must be right!** If we are to receive, we must thirst and we must pray. We cannot expect Him to give us the blessing until we are obedient. Our hearts must be free from condemnation *(I John 3:21-27)*.

As a candidate for this baptism, we must examine our motives and seek the Lord with a pure heart. A sanctifying work must be done in our lives so that we are free from the controlling influence of pride, from the negative power of bitterness, and from the destructive forces of anger and resentment. The **BELIEVER** must have a pure heart to be a **RECEIVER.**

(4) **The seeker must not allow discouragement!** Jesus tells the story in Luke 11:5 about a friend who arose and granted a neighbor his request

because the man continued to ask. If we keep asking and seeking and knocking, our request will be granted.

(5) **To receive, we must confess our weakness!** Too many of us tend to feel self-sufficient. We need spiritual power for spiritual living. The source of this power is in the Spirit of God. The **BAPTISM IN THE HOLY SPIRIT** brings a deeper relationship with the Lord, a wonderful sensitiveness to the things of God, a new dimension in prayer and praise, and permits us to be channels through which the Holy Spirit can manifest Himself in so many ways.

IS THIS THE DAY OF THE OUTPOURING OF THE HOLY SPIRIT?

God promised through the prophet Joel that He would pour out His Spirit in the "last days." For the past two thousand years (the last days), the Holy Spirit has been poured out. The Holy Spirit has been working throughout the entire church age. We have been promised a "former rain" and a "latter rain." God is moving on schedule. Everything fits into His divine program.

Today we are experiencing an increase in the ministry of the Holy Spirit. There are reasons why the outpouring is so evident today. Let me name some of these reasons:

(1) **The Holy Spirit has come to exalt the Lord Jesus Christ in an age of false teachers, false prophets, false Christs, and false religions.**

*"For there shall arise false Christs, and
false prophets, and shall show great signs
and wonders; insomuch that, if it were
possible, they shall deceive the very elect."*
Matthew 24:24

Jesus said:

*"Howbeit when he, the Spirit of truth,
is come, he will guide you into all truth:
for he shall not speak of himself; but whatsoever he shall hear, that shall he speak:
and he will show you things to come.*

*"He shall glorify me: for he shall receive
of mine, and shall show it unto you."*
John 16:13-14

On every side, we are seeing false teaching and
preaching of false gospel. To counteract the cult and
the occult, God is pouring out His Spirit across the
earth.

(2) **The Holy Spirit is being poured out to
counteract the Spirit of anti-Christ.** John told us
in his first letter that the spirit of anti-Christ was
working in the world already. Paul gave a special
warning to us.

*"Let no man deceive you by any means;
for that day shall not come, except there
come a falling away first, and that man of
sin be revealed, the son of perdition;*

*"Who opposeth and exalteth himself
about all that is called God...*

56

"For the mystery of iniquity doth already work: only he who now letteth will let, until he be taken out of the way.

"And then shall the Wicked be revealed, whom the Lord shall consume with the spirit of his mouth, and shall destroy with the brightness of his coming."
II Thessalonians 2:3-9

Deception is the tool that anti-Christ will use. Humanity will be conditioned to believe the great lie. Revival fire is spreading and gaining proportion. The revival is preparing a SPIRIT FILLED, SPIRIT ANOINTED, and SPIRIT LED church. The Holy Spirit is moving through the church to resist the deceptive powers of the spirit of anti-Christ.

(3) **The Holy Spirit is being poured out to counteract satanic activity and the flood of wickedness.** It is apparent that iniquity is abounding in these closing days. The Scriptures declare:

"But evil men and seducers shall wax worse and worse, deceiving, and being deceived."
II Timothy 3:13

There is a tidal wave of moral pollution. Pornography is sweeping across the world. Homosexuality is spreading like a cancer. Drug abuse has contaminated the nations. Witchcraft and devil worship are on the increase.

It is into this atmosphere that God promised that the Spirit of the Lord would lift up a standard (Isaiah 59:18).

(4) **The Holy Spirit is being poured out to ready the church for the coming of Christ.** The Father has sent the Holy Spirit into the world to seek a bride for Jesus Christ. Believers are on their way to a marriage celebration. It is the ministry of the Holy Spirit to work in the lives of believers...to present a spotless church as a bride adorned for the bridegroom.

(5) **It is the purpose of the Holy Spirit to bring in the greatest harvest of souls the Church has ever seen.** James referred to this time when he wrote:

> *"Be patient therefore, brethren, unto the coming of the Lord. Behold, the husbandman waiteth for the precious fruit of the earth, and hath long patience for it, until he receive the early and latter rain."*
> *James 5:7*

The doors are open! It is harvest time across the world!! It is time for the church to move beyond its own walls and reach out to a world that is ready to receive Christ. This is the church's greatest hour!

THE GIFTS OF THE SPIRIT

A distinction must be made between the Holy Spirit sent as a "gift" and the "gifts of the Holy Spirit." The following distinctives must be understood:

(1) The Holy Spirit as a Person being sent to indwell believers.

(2) The Holy Spirit baptizing us into the Body of Christ.

(3) The Lord baptizing us into the Holy Spirit.

(4) The gifts of the Spirit (spirituals) operating in the life of a believer (I Corinthians 12).

When we receive the Holy Spirit, He comes as a gift (John 14:16-17; John 15:26-27; and John 16:7-15). The Holy Spirit is a Person and was sent as a gift.

Then there are "spirituals" that are referred to as the "gifts of the Holy Spirit." There are **nine** of them.

"Now there are diversities of gifts, but the same Spirit.

"And there are differences of administrations, but the same Lord.

"And there are diversities of operations, but it is the same God which worketh all in all.

"But the manifestation of the Spirit is given to every man to profit withal.

"For to one is given by the Spirit the word of wisdom; to another the word of knowledge by the same Spirit;

"To another faith by the same Spirit; to another the gifts of healing by the same Spirit;

"To another the working of miracles; to another prophecy; to another discerning of spirits; to another divers kinds of tongues; to another the interpretation of tongues:

"But all these worketh that one and the selfsame Spirit, dividing to every man severally as he will."
I Corinthians 12:4-11

The person who has not received the **BAPTISM IN THE HOLY SPIRIT** cannot become the channel through which these gifts can function. They are referred to as the "manifestations of the spirit." Where people believe in and have received the experience of the BAPTISM IN THE HOLY SPIRIT, there will be evidences of the gifts of the spirit in their midst.

The Apostle Paul introduces this subject in I Corinthians 12:1 when he writes, **"Now concerning spirituals, brethren, I do not want you to be unlearned."** He then writes chapters 12, 13, and 14 on the subject of manifestations, spirituals, or the gifts of the spirit, and concludes by saying in I Corinthians 14:38, **"If any man be unlearned, let him be so."**

Very candidly, the apostle was saying, **"I have just spent three chapters talking about these manifestations. If you choose to be without knowledge after I have shared this revelation, then there is nothing more that I can do about it."** God wants us to have knowledge of the gifts, and the Holy Spirit wants these manifestations to be evident among believers.

When we have a good perspective on the work and ministry of the Holy Spirit, the things of the Lord are beautiful, powerful, and practical. The Holy Spirit came to give life and liberty to the believers! The Holy Spirit was sent so that those of us who desire to serve the Lord could be **ANOINTED** to do so.

We have been commanded to be **FILLED** with the Spirit so that the fruit of the Spirit could be produced in our lives. Christian character is developed to the degree that we stay FILLED. The Holy Spirit pours out blessing after blessing to inspire us to worship and praise. We are blessed because we are loved.

The Lord desires that every believer receive the BAPTISM IN THE HOLY SPIRIT.

This opens the doors to spiritual manifestations, to praying and praising in an unknown tongue, and to be used of the Lord in the power and demonstration of the Holy Spirit.

He is here to glorify the Lord Jesus Christ and to make us witnesses to the four corners of the earth.

My prayer is that YOU experience how REAL the Holy Spirit can be in YOUR life and ministry.

For further information, or for a book and tape catalog of **Dr. Paul E. Paino,** *please write:*

Paul E. Paino Ministries
P.O. Box 12205
Fort Wayne, IN 46863-2205